CONTENTS

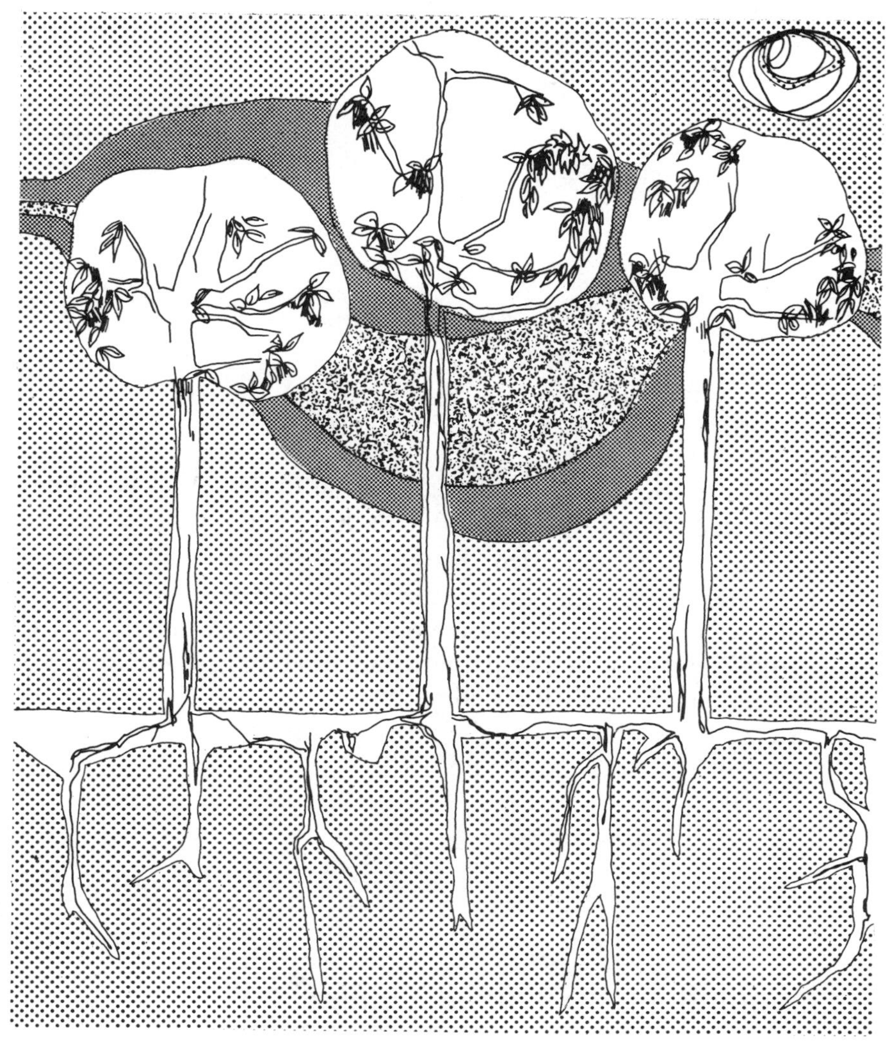

the spell of words

BY ELSIE T. RAK

Educators Publishing Service, Inc.
Cambridge and Toronto

Specific language disability (developmental dyslexia) is becoming more widely recognized. As a result, many high school and college students with this problem have been identified. The need for teaching matter at this level is evident. This speller contains methods and materials developed over a number of years of teaching these young men and women. While it is directed specifically toward people with this disability, it would be of value to anyone who has trouble with spelling.

Educators Publishing Service, Inc.
75 Moulton Street, Cambridge, Massachusetts 02138-1104

 Printed in U.S.A. ISBN 0-8388-0155-2

The Three Great Rules

THE DOUBLING RULE – or ONE, ONE, ONE

CHAPTER 1

What is a syllable? It is one push of breath. How many syllables are there in the word **push**? How many in your first name? In your last name? In the words **Maine, Vermont, Nevada, Wyoming, Texas, Florida, Washington, Utah?**

Look at these words:
ship, hot, grim
They are alike in three ways.

1. How many syllables do they have? . . . . **One** syllable.
2. What is at the end of each word? . . . . **One** consonant.
3. What is before the consonant? . . . . **One** vowel.

ONE **ONE** **ONE**

Look at this word:
ship + er = shipper
What has happened to the **p**? It has doubled.

Likewise: **ship + ing = shipping**
hot + er = hotter
grim + est = grimmest

But: **grim + ly = grimly**

The **m** in **grimly** did not double. Look at the two endings on **grim**. How do they differ? **Est** starts with a vowel, and the *m* is doubled. **Ly** starts with a consonant, and the **m** is not doubled.

This doubling rule is a two-way street. First look at the base word to see whether it is **One, One, One** (one syllable ending in one consonant after one vowel). Then look at the ending to see whether it begins with a vowel. If these conditions are met, double the final consonant in the base word. If either of these conditions is not met, then the doubling rule does not apply.

Combine these base words and endings: y as an ending beginning with a vowel

Copy the word, saying each letter as you write it:

ship + ing	**shipping**	shipping
ship + ment	**shipment**	shipment
hot + est	hottest	hottest
hot + ly	hotly	hotly
slop + y	sloppy	sloppy
mad + er	madder	madder
rob + er	robber	robber
star + y	starry	starry
fat + er	fatter	fatter
fog + y	foggy	foggy
wit + ness	wittness	witness
grin + ing	grinning	grinning
mad + ly	madly	madly

Use two of the above words in sentences:

____

____

____

____

Look again at:
hot + er = hotter
But: **cold + er = colder**

Why didn't the **d** in **cold** double?
Because this word does not fit the
One, One, One Rule.
It ends with two consonants.

Likewise: **weed + ing = weeding**

Again, why didn't the **d** double?
Because **weed** has two vowels.
It is not One, One, One.

Exercise 2

Combine these base words and endings:		Repeat the word, saying each letter as you write it:
bad + ly	**badly**	badly
trim + er	**trimmer**	trimmer
farm + ing	**farming**	farming
dust + y	dusty	dusty
flop + y	floppy	floppy
rent + ed	rented	rented
sun + y	sunny	sunny
fright + en	frighten	frighten
blot + er	blotter	blotter
fib + ing	fibbing	fibbing
win + some	winsome	winsome

fit + ful	fitful	fitful
grit + y	gritty	gritty
sad + en	sadden	sadden
sail + ing	sailing	sailing spoiling
rest + less	restless	restless
red + ish	reddish	reddish
bag + age	baggage	baggage
garb + age	garbage	garbage
win + ing	winning	winning
good + ness	goodness	goodness
snap + y	snappy	snappy
help + er	helper	helper
quit + ing	quitting	quitting
flat + ly	flatly	flatly
slim + er	slimmer	slimmer
cold + est	coldest	coldest

Use three of the above words in sentences:

Exercise 3

Do you notice that you are also learning to spell endings? These endings can be used on a thousand words, and they are always spelled the same. Isn't that a boon? Learn them once and use them countless times in your life. Notice especially the **ending** <u>**ful.**</u> The **word** is **full**: A glass full of milk. List all of the endings you have used so far:

Exercise 4

Add the above endings to the words below:
Employ as many different ones as possible.

As you copy,
say each letter:

bag
mop
child
cook
grip
bold
glad
sad
big
prig

seem ______ ______

mud ______ ______

wood ______ ______

clip ______ ______

blot ______ ______

nail ______ ______

pack ______ ______

Exercise 5

Add these endings: Say the letters as you write:

feed + ing ______ ______

lug + age ______ ______

sod + en ______ ______

swift + er ______ ______

band + age ______ ______

wet + ness ______ ______

slip + er ______ ______

quit + ing ______ ______

dim + ing ______ ______

dim + ly ______ ______

scrub + ed ______ ______

risk + y ______ ______

stub + y stubby ____________

fiend + ish friendish ____________

snap + y snappy ____________

snob + ish snobbish ____________

Composition 1

Choose a small technique and describe it so precisely that any fool who follows your instructions can do it. Examples: how to start an outboard motor; how to insert a lens in the eye. Don't use these examples, but think of a technique on your own.

Composition 2

How do you get from your home to school or work? Include distance, right and left directions, street names, and transportation in your paper.

The Three Great Rules

THE SILENT E RULE

CHAPTER 2

In the word **blame** the **e** is silent. Its function is to make the **a** long.

blame + ing = blaming

What has happened to the **e**?
It is dropped.
The ending begins with a vowel.

But: **blame + less = blameless**

The **e** is not dropped.
The ending begins with a consonant.

Likewise: **use + ing = using**
use + ful = useful

like + ing = liking
like + ly = likely

late + er = later
late + ness = lateness

A word ending in a silent **e** drops the **e** before an ending beginning with a vowel but does not change before an ending beginning with a consonant.

Exercise 1

Join these words and endings:		Repeat, saying each letter as you write it:
hope + ing	**hoping**	__________
hope + ful	**hopeful**	__________

dine + ing

write + ing

tune + ful

shine + y

time + er

hope + less

take + ing

sore + ness

flame + ing

fame + ous

care + ing

dive + ing

shade + y

noise + less

erase + er

type + ing

tire + some

Use two of the above words in sentences:

Comparing the Doubling Rule and the Silent E Rule

To compare the Doubling Rule and the Silent E Rule, consider these words:

scrap + **ing** = **scrapping** (doubling)
scrape + **ing** = **scraping** (Silent E)

The double **p** indicates a short **a.** The single **p** indicates a long **a** at the end of an open syllable. An open syllable is one that ends with a vowel. The vowel is usually long: **Po lish.** A closed syllable is one in which the vowel is followed by a consonant: **pol ish.** The vowel is usually short. (See Chapter 3)

Exercise 2

Read these words aloud:

capped	skidding	matter	ripped	hopper	rider
caper	bidding	matting	slimming	shipping	cutter
capping	biding	mated	slimy	shaping	cuter
sitting	bidder	biting	slimmer	shipped	cutting
sited	hiding	bitter	shining	shaped	filling
sitter	hidden	biter	shinning	shaper	filed
sloping	taping	scared	shinned	coping	filing
slipping	tapping	scarred	shiny	copped	filled
slipper	taped	scaring	hoping	copper	moping
sloppy	tapped	scarring	hopping	riding	mopping
sloped	tapper	ripping	hoped	ridding	mopped
sliding	mating	riper	hopped	ridden	moped

Join these words and endings:	Copy, saying each letter as you write it:
engage + ment	
active + ity	
adventure + ous	
revolve + ing	
combine + ation	
repulse + ive	
distaste + ful	
admire + ation	
expense + ive	
virtue + ous	
endure + ance	
extreme + ly	
quote + ation	
replace + ment	
decorate + ive	
declare + ation	
rare + ity	
disgrace + ful	
create + ive	

engrave + ing engraving ______

amaze + ment amazement ______

elevate + or elevator ______

Use three of these words in sentences:

ment ing ful y er

some ness less ous ly

ive ation ity ance ed

Exercise 4

List all of the endings you have used so far.

Exercise 5

Use a variety of the above endings on these words:

Copy, saying the letters as you write them:

move movement ______

debate debating ______

lone lonely ______

lame lamer

place placement

trade traded

believe believing

abuse abusive

nerve nervous

examine examimed

tumble tumbling

amuse amusement

love lover

slime slimeless

grieve grieving

pure purely

life lifeless

brave bravely

wide wider

Exercise 6

Combining the Doubling Rule and the Silent E Rule

Join these words and endings:

Copy, saying each letter as you write it:

scrub + ing	scrubbing	scrubbing
steam + er	steamer	steamer

dive + ing ______ ______

milk + ed ______ ______

pop + ing ______ ______

mad + ness ______ ______

haze + y ______ ______

shame + less ______ ______

telephone + ing ______ ______

hid + en ______ ______

snoop + ing ______ ______

trouble + some ______ ______

ripe + ness ______ ______

Exceptions to the Silent E Rule

1. With a few endings, keep **c** or **g** soft by retaining the **e.** For example:

peaceable	serviceable	exchangeable	courageous
replaceable	enforceable	chargeable	outrageous
traceable	vengeance	manageable	advantageous
noticeable	changeable	salvageable	

2. Save yourself a lot of trouble by memorizing these exceptions:

wholly duly truly awful argument judgment acknowledgment

While you are at it, you might as well learn **ninth.**

3. Some words lose their identity without the **e.**

dyeing	You may like **dyeing** your hair but no one likes **dying** in the gutter.
singeing	Not **singing**
tingeing	What is **tinging?**
hoeing	**Hoing, toing, canoing, shoing** are nonsense.
canoeing	
shoeing	
mileage	
acreage	

Composition 1

Describe a favorite spot.

Composition 2

If you had three months of free time and money were no problem, where on this earth would you go, and why?

Composition 3

Write a letter of complaint to one of the big oil companies about the service at one of its gas stations. Choose the writer of the letter and the circumstances, and write from that point of view (a middle-aged person who always complains anyway, a doctor in a hurry, a couple on a date, etc.).

Composition 4

You are a public relations director of the oil company. Answer the preceding letter.

Syllable Division and Accent

CHAPTER 3

It is of vast help in both reading and spelling to be able to divide words into syllables. At the same time, accent should be stressed. Many students with developmental dyslexia have extreme difficulty with it. Accent is necessary for reading and recognizing long words and for the second half of the doubling rule:

A syllable is one push of breath.

One-syllable words:
ham, cat, run, hut, hope, big, place,
bring, tramp, scrape, drown, pond, like

Two-syllable words:
window, baseball, rented, bigger,
hopeful, bringing, trampled

Three-syllable words:
likable, enjoyment, refreshing, rewarded

Syllable Division I

If a word of two syllables contains two consonants surrounded by two vowels, divide between the consonants:

confound	con found
extent	ex tent
triplets	trip lets

Divide into syllables:

absent ____________ ____________

intense ____________ ____________

winter ____________ ____________

absorb ____________ ____________

perfect ____________ ____________

always ____________ ____________

consult ____________ ____________

shipment ____________ ____________

burlap ____________ ____________

confirm ____________ ____________

lentil ____________ ____________

gasket ____________ ____________

insist ____________ ____________

cactus ____________ ____________

admit ____________ ____________

faster ____________ ____________

invent ____________ ____________

tractor ____________ ____________

admire ____________ ____________

survive ____________ ____________

Accent

In English we usually bear down more heavily on one syllable than on another. To determine which syllable has the accent, hammer on each in turn with a loud bang:

con found

Is it **CON found** or is it **con FOUND?**

Shout if necessary.
It is **con FOUND.**
Mark the accented syllable thus: **con fóund.**

ex tent

Is it **EX tent** or **ex TENT?**
It is **ex tent.**

trip lets

TRIP lets or **trip LETS?**
It is **trip lets.**

Exercise 2

Return to Exercise 1 and mark the accented syllables in the list.

Syllable Division II

If a word of two syllables contains a double consonant surrounded by vowels, it follows that the word is divided between the double letters:

slipper	slíp per
annoy	an nóy

Exercise 3

Divide into syllables and accent:

immune	________	________	little	________	________
mattress	________	________	comma	________	________
letter	________	________	access	________	________
rattan	________	________	fossil	________	________
summit	________	________	peddler	________	________
annul	________	________			

Syllable Division III

An open syllable ends with a vowel, usually long:

pro vóke	(prō)
é qual	(ē)
u níte	(ū)
re móte	(rė̄)

A closed syllable ends with a consonant; the vowel is usually short:

vắl ue	(vǎl)
Lắt in	(Lǎt)
tĕ́n or	(tĕn)

If you have a word of two syllables with only one consonant surrounded by vowels, as above, the problem is to divide them properly. To solve it, you simply try both ways until you recognize the word:

Try it first as an open syllable ending in a long vowel:

lē vel

There is no such word.

Now try it as a closed syllable and a short vowel:

lĕv el

Recognize it?

Similarly: **pā nel** No
pǎn el Yes
vā por Yes
vǎp or No

Exercise 4

Divide into syllables and accent:

chapel	________	________	legal	________	________
regain	________	________	provide	________	________
stupid	________	________	vigor	________	________
acid	________	________	pilot	________	________
bonus	________	________	exile	________	________
omit	________	________	obey	________	________

visit	________	________	motor	________	________
novel	________	________	profit	________	________

Exercise 5

Divide into syllables and accent:

inner	________	________	making	________	________
admit	________	________	ballad	________	________
posing	________	________	litter	________	________
entire	________	________	rover	________	________
robin	________	________	market	________	________
adding	________	________	suffer	________	________

Syllable Division IV

There are many words ending in a consonant + le. The **ble, tle, dle** etc. are syllables. For example:

rid dle   trem ble   i dle   tur tle   tram ple

Composition 1

You are in the hospital. Write a thank-you note to someone for a specific gift.

Composition 2

You are still in the hospital. Write a letter to a friend with whom you can be frank and tell her exactly what you think of various hospital procedures.

The Three Great Rules

THE Y RULE

CHAPTER 4

What do these words have in common?

spy, defy, noisy

They all end in y.
What is before the y?
A consonant.

spy + ed = spied
defy + ance = defiance

The **y** changes to **i**
when the ending begins
with a vowel.

noisy + ly = noisily

The **y** changes to **i**
when the ending begins
with a consonant.

This is an "all or nothing" rule. It doesn't matter how the ending begins. If a word ends in **y** preceded by a consonant, the **y** always changes to **i**.

But: **spy + ing = spying**
defy + ing = defying

Only before the ending **ing** is the **y** retained. The reason is that you can't have two **i**'s together in English. (**Ski** was recently stolen from Norwegian. You can go **skiing**, but don't go any further than that with two **i**'s.)

What do these words have in common?

pray, buy, pay

They all end in y.
What is before the y?
A vowel.

pray + ed = prayed
buy + er = buyer
pay + able = payable

The y does not change.

pay + ment = payment

The y does not change.

pay + ing = paying

The y does not change.

Again, it is all or nothing. It doesn't matter how the ending begins. If a word ends in y preceded by a vowel, the y <u>never</u> changes.

Exercise 1

Add these endings:

Copy, saying the letters as you write them:

cry + ed	____________	____________
rely + ance	____________	____________
pray + er	____________	____________
worry + ing	____________	____________
joy + ful	____________	____________
enjoy + ment	____________	____________
say + ing	____________	____________

sleepy + ness ______________________ ______________________

glory + ous ______________________ ______________________

delay + ed ______________________ ______________________

merry + est ______________________ ______________________

study + ing ______________________ ______________________

busy + ness ______________________ ______________________

lonely + ness ______________________ ______________________

pay + able ______________________ ______________________

carry + ed ______________________ ______________________

hurry + ing ______________________ ______________________

stray + ed ______________________ ______________________

fly + er ______________________ ______________________

supply + ed ______________________ ______________________

healthy + er ______________________ ______________________

smoky + ness ______________________ ______________________

spy + ing ______________________ ______________________

Exercise 2

Add these endings:

Repeat, saying the letters as you write them:

bray + ed ______________________ ______________________

bray + ing ______________________ ______________________

funny + est ______________________ ______________________

comply + ance ______________________ ______________________

tiny + er ______________________ ______________________

melody + ous ______________________ ______________________

injury + ous ______________________ ______________________

crafty + ness ______________________ ______________________

multiply + ed ______________________ ______________________

multiply + ing ______________________ ______________________

envy + ous ______________________ ______________________

apply + ance ______________________ ______________________

destroy + ing ______________________ ______________________

victory + ous ______________________ ______________________

enjoy + able ______________________ ______________________

merry + ment ______________________ ______________________

mystery + ous ______________________ ______________________

beauty + ful ______________________ ______________________

vary + ous ______________________ ______________________

employ + ment ______________________ ______________________

dismay + ed ______________________ ______________________

moody + ly ______________________ ______________________

mercy + ful ______________________ ______________________

Exercise 3

Make a list of the endings used in the two preceding exercises:

____

____

____

____

Exercise 4

Add the above endings to these words:	Copy, saying the letters as you write them:
relay ______________	______________
easy ______________	______________
happy ______________	______________
pity ______________	______________
justify ______________	______________
delay ______________	______________
dusty ______________	______________
ready ______________	______________
dainty ______________	______________
industry ______________	______________
heavy ______________	______________
prey ______________	______________

copy ______________________ ______________________

fancy ______________________ ______________________

fortify ______________________ ______________________

buy ______________________ ______________________

steady ______________________ ______________________

Exercise 5

Samples from all three rules:

trouble + some ______________________ ______________________

replace + ment ______________________ ______________________

carry + ed ______________________ ______________________

star + y ______________________ ______________________

shine + y ______________________ ______________________

debate + able ______________________ ______________________

skin + y ______________________ ______________________

intense + ly ______________________ ______________________

wit + ness ______________________ ______________________

wealthy + est ______________________ ______________________

hurry + ing ______________________ ______________________

educate + or ______________________ ______________________

loaf + er ______________________ ______________________

strap + ing	____________	____________
tame + ly	____________	____________
lucky + ly	____________	____________
wood + en	____________	____________
fib + ing	____________	____________
guide + ance	____________	____________
duty + ful	____________	____________
price + less	____________	____________
spite + ful	____________	____________
fury + ous	____________	____________
endure + able	____________	____________
shut + ers	____________	____________

Exceptions to the Y Rule

lay	laid
say	said
pay	paid
slay	slain
day	daily
gay	gaily or gayly

These words retain y before **ly** and **ness**, but otherwise usually follow the rule:

shy	shyly	shyness	shier	shiest
sly	slyly	slyness	slier	sliest
spry	spryly	spryness	sprier	spriest
wry	wryly	wryness	wrier	wriest
dry	dryly	dryness	drier	driest

Composition 1

Describe the room you sleep in.

Composition 2

If you had $100 to spend on this room, what would you do to improve it?

The Three Great Rules

THE DOUBLING RULE – Part 2

CHAPTER 5

The doubling rule applies to words of one syllable: one syllable, ending in one consonant, after one vowel.

Look at these words of more than one syllable:

omit + ed = omitted
compel + ing = compelling

mit ends in one consonant
after one vowel.
The **t** is doubled.

pel ends in one consonant
after one vowel.
The **l** is doubled.

But: **suffer + ed = suffered**
number + ing = numbering

What is the difference between **omit** and **suffer**? In **omit** the accent is on the last syllable. In **suffer** the accent is **not** on the last syllable.

In words of more than one syllable, if the accent is on the final syllable and that syllable fits the other conditions of the doubling rule, the final consonant is doubled.

Exercise 1

Add these endings:

Copy, saying each letter as you write it:

admit + ance ______**admittance**______ ____________________

pilot + ing ______**piloting**______ ____________________

forgot + en ____________________ ____________________

profit + able ____________ ____________

incur + ed ____________ ____________

unforget + able ____________ ____________

limit + ed ____________ ____________

blunder + ing ____________ ____________

disbar + ed ____________ ____________

market + able ____________ ____________

Look at these words:
consist + ent = consistent

The accent is on the last syllable, but it ends in **two** consonants.

reveal + ing = revealing

The accent is on the last syllable, but the final consonant is preceded by **two** vowels.

equip + ed = equipped
equip + ment = equipment

ed begins with a vowel; therefore, the **p** is doubled.

ment begins with a consonant; the **p** is not doubled.

For a word of more than one syllable **all** of the conditions of the doubling rule must be met, and the accent must be on the last syllable. Then the final consonant is doubled.

Exercise 2

Add these endings:

Copy, saying each letter as you write it:

forbid + en ____________ ____________

appear + ance ____________ ____________

allot + ment ______________________ ______________________

contain + ing ______________________ ______________________

defend + ant ______________________ ______________________

excel + ent ______________________ ______________________

resent + ful ______________________ ______________________

regret + able ______________________ ______________________

garden + ing ______________________ ______________________

perform + ance ______________________ ______________________

enter + ed ______________________ ______________________

offer + ing ______________________ ______________________

acquit + al ______________________ ______________________

consult + ant ______________________ ______________________

deliver + ed ______________________ ______________________

prefer + ing ______________________ ______________________

abhor + ent ______________________ ______________________

Exercise 3

List all the endings used in Exercises 1 and 2:

________ ________ ________ ________ ________ ________ ________

________ ________ ________ ________ ________ ________ ________

Exercise 4

Add the above endings to these words, using as much variety as possible:

Copy, saying each letter as you write it:

commit ______________________ ______________________

recover ______________________ ______________________

propel ______________________ ______________________

prevent ______________________ ______________________

concur ______________________ ______________________

gather ______________________ ______________________

transmit ______________________ ______________________

subtract ______________________ ______________________

forget ______________________ ______________________

incur ______________________ ______________________

limit ______________________ ______________________

Exercise 5

Join these words and endings:

Copy, saying each letter as you write it:

control + able ______________________ ______________________

conceal + ing ______________________ ______________________

incur + ed ______________________ ______________________

defer + ment ______________________ ______________________

begin + ing ______________________ ______________________

remit + ance ______________________ ______________________

contend + ed ______________________ ______________________

annul + ment ______________________ ______________________

befit + ing ______________________ ______________________

respect + ing ______________________ ______________________

occur + ence ______________________ ______________________

subsist + ence ______________________ ______________________

admit + ance ______________________ ______________________

repent + ance ______________________ ______________________

quarrel + ing ______________________ ______________________

Use three of the above words in sentences:

____

____

____

____

Composition 1

What, in your opinion, is the best choice of a car for a woman in her early twenties? Give your reasons.

Composition 2

Best choice for a family car.

Word Building

PREFIXES AND SUFFIXES

CHAPTER 6

You have already begun to build words by adding endings:

joy **ful**
joy **ous**

Try adding at each end:

en joy **ment**
en joy **able**

What can you do with **light**?

light
light **er**
light **ing**
light **ning**
en light **en**
de light
de light **ed**
de light **ful**
de light **ful ly**

With **camp**?

camp **ing**
de camp
en camp **ment**

And **count**?

count
count **er**
en count **er**
count **er act**
un count **ed**

A prefix is something fastened to the beginning of a word and a suffix is something fastened to the end. Together they are affixes (fastened to).

The Anglo-Saxon Prefix a

The Anglo-Saxon prefix **a** is an unaccented **a**, a slur, a grunt, a schwa(ə), meaning "on, in, at." It is used with many short familiar words:

abed	aboard	around
about	adrift	asleep
aloud	amid	apiece
arise	alone	away
arouse	afar	aware
abide	aground	awhile
above	alive	ajar
across	alike	

Latin Prefixes

a) **Con** is a Latin prefix meaning "with." That is all you need to memorize.

confirm	control	consent
connect	construct	continue
conduct	contain	confront
contrive	confer	converse

But:

cor rect	com pose
col lide	com bine
com mend	co operate

These are still the prefix **con**, but what has happened to the **n**? It has changed to match the beginning of the root because the word has a pleasanter sound and is easier to say.

b) Consider the prefix **ad**, meaning "to":

advance admire adhere admit

But:

af firm	ag gravate
ap praise	an nounce
al low	ar rest
ac quire	as sert
ac cord	am munition
ac cept	at tain
ac knowledge	

All you need to remember is how to spell **ad**, meaning "to." If you hear a sound other than **d** you know the **d** has been changed. The effect is to look like a doubling.

c) Here is a list of familiar Latin prefixes used with the root **pose** (from the French word meaning "to place")

ad (af, ap, al, ac, ag, an, ar, am, as, at): to, toward	apposition
con (cor, col, com, co): with	compose
dis (di, dif): apart from	dispose
de: down, from	depose
ex (ec, ef, e): out	expose
in (im, il, ir): in, not	impose
inter (intel, intro): among, between	interpose
ob (oc, of, op, o): against	oppose
per: through	
pre: before	presuppose
pro: forth, before	propose
re: back, again	repose (**re + pausare, "to rest"**)
sub (suc, suf, sup, sum): below, under	suppose
trans (traf, tra): across, beyond	transpose

Exercise 1

Make a list of words using the above prefixes and the root **port**, meaning "to carry." And don't forget **carport**.

__________ __________ __________ __________ __________ __________ __________

__________ __________ __________ __________ __________ __________ __________

__________ __________ __________ __________ __________ __________ __________

effect
defect

Why are there two f's in effect and only one in **defect**? **Effect** has the prefix **ex**, with the **x** changed to **f** to go with the root. **Defect** has the prefix **de**, which has nothing to change. It ends in a vowel which can easily be pronounced with **fect**.

accommodate
recommend

Each of these words has two prefixes. Accommodate has two **c**'s: the **d** in **ad** is changed to a **c** to go with **con**. It also has two **m**'s: the **n** in **con** is changed to **m** to go with the root (**modus**, meaning "a measure").

Recommend has one **c** because the prefix is **re**, which does not have a consonant to be changed. It also has two **m**'s: the **n** in **con** is changed to **m** to match the root (**mandare**, meaning "commit"). Many naturally good spellers have trouble with these double letters because they do not know the logic behind the spelling.

Exercise 2

Make a list of words using **script** and **scrib** ("write"), **cept** ("take"), **tract** ("draw"), and **ject** ("throw").

Ject is easy. Probably everyone has suffered an **injection**, and done a science **project** and held an **object** in their hands, and studied **adjectives**, and knows that pilots can **eject** themselves from a plane, and in this space age seen a **projectile**. What other **ject** words are there?

script, scrib	**cept**	**tract**	**ject**
____________	____________	____________	____________
____________	____________	____________	____________
____________	____________	____________	____________
____________	____________	____________	____________
____________	____________	____________	____________
____________	____________	____________	____________
____________	____________	____________	____________
____________	____________	____________	____________

More Latin Prefixes

se: away from, apart	seclude
ne (neg): not	neglect
super (sur): above	superimpose
ab: from	absolve
circum: around	circumscribe
intro (intra): within	introvert
ante: before	antedate

cede, cess

Cede (from **cedere,** meaning "to yield") is spelled **cede** in all words except **exceed, succeed, and proceed.** Memorize this sentence and keep out of trouble: He proc**ee**ded to succ**ee**d in exc**ee**ding the speed limit. **Supersede** comes from a different root: **sedere**, meaning "sit."

Exercise 3

Build two lists of words using **cede** and **cess.** Also take the root cess, use **ne** as a prefix and either **ity** or **ary** as a suffix. This may be a revelation to you.

cede **cess**

fer, lat

Fer and **lat** come from **ferre**, meaning "to bear." When you add the suffix **ence** to **fer**, you do not double the **r**. Other exceptions are **preferable, referable, transferable.**

Exercise 4

Make lists of words with **fer** and **lat**; **pel** and **puls** ("drive"); **spec**, **spect**, and **spic** ("look").

fer, lat	pel, puls	spec, spect, spic
____________	____________	____________
____________	____________	____________
____________	____________	____________
____________	____________	____________
____________	____________	____________

Anglo-Saxon Prefixes

un: not	unhappy	
for: away, against	forbid	
fore: before, ahead	forecast	
in: in, into	inland	Why does **misspell** have two s's?
mis: wrong	mistake	
out: beyond	outlaw	
under: below	underrate	Why does **underrate** have two **r**'s?

Greek Prefixes

phil: love	philanthropy
pan: all	panacea
peri: around	perimeter
syn: together	syncopate
tele: far	telephone
poly: many	polyglot

Exercise 5

Find another word for each of the Anglo-Saxon and Greek prefixes:

____________ ____________ ____________

A Few More Latin Roots

fac, fect: make or do	facility, affect
form: form	conform
sect: cut	bisect
part: part	participate
viv, vit: live	vivisection, devitalize
duc, duct: lead	viaduct
cid, cis: cut, kill	germicide, precision
pend, pens: hang	suspension
leg: law	legislature
mis, mit: send	committee

Exercise 6

Find another word for each of the above roots. By this time roots should be popping out of the page at you as you read.

Composition 1

Write a letter to your newspaper describing a traffic hazard that should be corrected.

Composition 2

Write a letter to your insurance company describing a car accident you had. If you have not had one, describe one you have seen.

A Sound Principle

G and C; GE and DGE;
CH and TCH; K and CK;
WORDS ENDING in BLE, DLE, etc.

CHAPTER 7

G and **C**: There are two sounds for the letter **c**—/k/ and /s/— and for the letter **g**—/g/ and /j/.

c is hard – /k/ – before **a**, **o**, and **u**:

candy
cot
cut

c is soft – /s/ – before **e**, **i**, and **y**:

cement
cycle
circle

To get the hard sound of **c** – /k/ –
before **e**, **i**, or **y**, use the letter **k**:

keen
kick

g is usually soft – /j/ – before **e**, **i**, and **y**:

germ
ginger
energy

g is usually hard – /g/ – before **a**, **o**, and **u**:

gasp
got
gust

To get the soft sound of **g** – /j/ –
before **a**, **o**, and **u**, use the letter **j**:

jab
jot
jump

Note that the root **ject** ("throw") is spelled with the letter **j**: project, interjection.

GE and **DGE**: The sound of /j/ at the end of a one-syllable word and in the middle or end of a few two-syllable words is spelled **ge** or **dge**. It is a very simple matter to choose which to use.

In English the short vowels are weak and need something to lean on. Give them that extra **d**:

pledge
bridge
judge

Endings can be put on these words:

pudgy
badger
lodging

If the short vowel has some other letter to lean on, use **ge**:

singe
plunge

This principle applies to short vowels only. For other vowel sounds use **ge**:

rage
large
forge
gouge

Two-syllable words:

midget	hodgepodge
fidget	knowledge
gadget	cartridge
budget	partridge
	porridge

Exercise 1

Fill in with **ge** or **dge**:

le________	stran________	smu________
bar________	gor________	do________
bri________	bin________	plun________
we________	dre________	e________
ca________	fu________	ba________
gru________	wa________	gou________

Fill in with **ge** or **dge**:

he__________	ran__________	frin__________
gau__________	sta__________	ri__________
for__________	le__________	ra__________
ca__________	ur__________	ple__________
bul__________	tru__________	

CH and **TCH**: The sound /ch/ at the end of a syllable or a word is spelled **ch** or **tch**. The same principle you learned for **ge** and **dge** applies here:

If the short vowel stands alone, use **tch**:

patch
pitchfork
clutch
stitch

If the short vowel has some other letter to lean on, use **ch**:

lunch
pinch
bench

This principle concerns short vowels only. Other vowel sounds take **ch**:

porch
march
slouch
coach

Exceptions:

rich
which
much
such

sandwich
attach
detach
ostrich
butcher

Learn them. . .

Exercise 3

Fill in with **ch** or **tch**:

ma ________	ca ________	la ________
per ________	scra ________	chur ________
wi ________	prea ________	sna ________
ran ________	hi ________	pi ________
lyn ________	por ________	mun ________

Exercise 4

Fill in with **ch** or **tch**:

bun ________	ri ________	no ________
su ________	wre ________	whi ________
Sco ________	hun ________	ki ________en
cru ________	sandwi ________	ske ________
stre ________	wren ________	ha ________et
tor ________	grou ________	sten ________
it ________	mu ________	scor ________
poa ________	hi ________	di ________

Exercise 5

Dictation 44 is a description of a picture. Draw a diagram of it, putting everything mentioned in the proper spot.

K and **CK**: The sound /k/ at the end of a one-syllable word preceded by a short vowel is spelled **k** or **ck**. The same principle you learned for **ge** and **dge**, **ch** and **tch** helps you choose which to use.

If the short vowel is alone, use **ck**:

pick
pack
rock
buck

If the short vowel has some other letter to lean on, use **k**:

milk
dusk
plank

This principle applies to short vowels only. Other vowel sounds take **k**:

beak
park
lake

Exercise 6

Fill in with **k** or **ck**:

plu __________	ba __________	lo __________
spar __________	bar __________	stin __________
lea __________	bea __________	smo __________ e
li __________	bu __________	mas __________
lar __________	bun __________	lu __________
sa __________	ra __________	spe __________
see __________	ree __________	por __________
bul __________	ran __________	

Exercise 7

Fill in with **k** or **ck**:

dar___en	so___et
pa___age	co___pit
dus___	blan___et
ho___ey	cri___et
mar___et	re___less
ma___erel	tan___er
ti___et	stri___en
sil___	cra___er
co___ney	ti___lish
bu___et	ro___et
sli___er	bun___er
ja___et	ha___ney

Other Ways of Spelling the Sound /k/.

The Greek way: words of Greek origin spell the sound /k/ with **ch.**

The French Way: some words of French origin end with the sound /k/ spelled **que.**

Exercise 8

Copy, saying each letter as you write it.

ache (Anglo Saxon) ________	echo ________
school ________	architect ________
scholar ________	mechanical ________
chorus ________	technical ________
character ________	chronology ________
Christmas ________	synchronize ________
choir ________	orchid ________
monarch ________	chaos ________
stomach ________	

scheme ______________________ psychology ______________________

schedule ______________________ psychiatry ______________________

Exercise 9

Copy, saying each letter as you write it:

antique ______________________ chair

unique ______________________ experiment

oblique ______________________ angle

clique exclusive ______________________

pique needless ______________________

technique delicate ______________________

critique literary ______________________

physique masculine ______________________

grotesque ______________________ figure

picturesque ______________________ scene

Words Ending in BLE, DLE, etc.

You now know how to choose **k** or **ck** to spell the sound /k/. This same principle applies to words ending in **kle** and **ckle**:

If the short vowel is alone, use **ckle**:

tackle
buckle

If the short vowel has something to lean on, use **kle**:

sprinkle
ankle

This principle applies to short vowels only. Other vowel sounds take **kle**:

sparkle

Further Examples:

wrinkle	knuckle
shackle	hackles
chuckle	rankle

This principle can be extended to double letters in words ending in **ble**, **ple**, **gle**, etc.

If the short vowel stands alone use a double letter:

babble
rubble
dribble

If the short vowel has something to lean on, use the single letter:

ramble
stumble

This principle applies to short vowels only. Other vowel sounds or spellings take the single letter:

marble
double
stable

Examples:

bubble
tremble
pebble
humble
able

amble
stubble
bobble
bumblebee
rumble

Likewise:

puddle
handle
needle
spindle
bridle
huddle
fiddle
muddle

hurdle
bundle
cuddle
candle
cradle
ladle
poodle
paddle

angle
goggles
giggle
bangle
toggle switch
juggle
bungle
tingle

gargle
spangle
struggle
strangle
wrangle
dangle
boggle
tangle

little
turtle
bottle
settle
bristle
bustle
mottle
nettle

hustle
whistle
mettle
mantle
thistle
fettle
gristle
scuttle

frazzle
dazzle
drizzle
fizzle
puzzle
grizzle
guzzle
hassle

rifle
riffle
muffle
ruffle
trifle
truffles
stifle
baffle
raffle

ripple
trample
people
ample

example
staple
simple
maple

sample
supple

Exception: triple

Composition 1

Standing at your front or back door, what do you see, hear and smell?

Composition 2

If you came into the kitchen for breakfast and found a firefighter's slicker and helmet on the table, how would you explain their presence?

The Old Saw

IE and EI

CHAPTER 8

There is a group of words in which the $/\bar{e}/$ sound is spelled **ie** or **ei**, not **ee**, **ea**, etc. The chief problem is to know when this spelling fits. The way to learn this is to work with the words long enough to have a suspicion in your mind that they belong to this group.

The old saw is helpful:

i before **e**
except after **c**
or when sounded like $\bar{a}$
as in neighbor and weigh.

I before **E**

grief	grieve	niece	field
belief	believe	priest	yield
relief	relieve	fiend	shield
chief	achieve		wield
thief	reprieve		
brief	retrieve		

siege	pier	diesel (engine)
fierce	tier	frontier
pierce	piece	cashier
shriek		

Copy the lists of words from the previous page:

Add endings if possible:

Except after **c**

ceiling	perceive
conceit	conceive
deceit	deceive
receipt	receive

Or when sounded like ā as in neighbor and weigh.

neighbor	vein	deign
weigh	skein	feign
neigh	rein	reign
weight	reindeer	beige
freight	heir	
eight	heiress	
eighteen	heirloom	
	their	

Exercise 2

Copy the above lists of words, saying the letters aloud as you write them:

____________ ____________ ____________ ____________

____________ ____________ ____________ ____________

____________ ____________ ____________ ____________

____________ ____________ ____________ ____________

____________ ____________ ____________ ____________

____________ ____________ ____________ ____________

____________ ____________ ____________

Fill in with **ie** or **ei**:

bel__f	ach__vement	br__f
perc__ve	d__sel	ch__f
s__ge	r__gn	w__gh
sk__n	p__ce	th__r
retr__ver	r__ndeer	sh__ld
c__ling	pr__st	n__ce
h__rloom	dec__ve	__ght

Exceptions:

either	seize
neither	seizure
leisure	weird
foreign	height

These words can be put into a silly sentence: **Neither leisured foreigner seized the weird heights.** Please learn it. You will save yourself a lot of trouble.

Other Exceptions:

caffein	forfeit
protein	counterfeit
sheik	

For the curious, or for those who love words, there are more lists in the back of this book.

Exercise 4

Fill in with **ie** or **ei**:

shr____k	h____ght	s____ve
b____ge	gr____vance	n____ghbor
fr____nd	v____n	h____r
n____ther	caff____n	dec____t
rec____ve	rel____f	cash____r
p____r	d____sel	repr____ve
prot____n	sh____k	fr____ght
th____f	f____gn	f____rce
for____gn	t____r	bel____vable
____ghty	s____ze	sh____ld
y____ld		

Composition 1

Describe an occasion when you were late and it mattered very much.

Composition 2

If you had to plan a birthday party for a ten-year-old boy and his friends, what would you do?

Some Useful Word Patterns

F, L and S
"ILD, OLD" WORDS
THE SOUND of U

CHAPTER 9

You probably know this without realizing it: words of one syllable ending in **f**, **l** or s generally double the **f**, **l** or s, as in **stuff**, **grass**, **smell**.

Exercise 1

Copy these words, saying each letter as you write it:

off	______________	hell	______________
staff	______________	knell	______________
cliff	______________	swell	______________
whiff	______________	cell	______________
sniff	______________	fell	______________
cuff	______________	well	______________
puff	______________	tell	______________
muff	______________	quill	______________
bluff	______________	kill	______________
brass	______________	fill	______________

class ______________________ bill ______________________

crass ______________________ drill ______________________

pass ______________________ pill ______________________

spill ______________________

skill ______________________

Exercise 2

Copy, repeating the letters:

dull ______________________ bliss ______________________

gull ______________________ hiss ______________________

hull ______________________ boss ______________________

mull ______________________ toss ______________________

chess ______________________ loss ______________________

mess ______________________ dross ______________________

press ______________________ cross ______________________

stress ______________________ moss ______________________

dress ______________________ fuss ______________________

less ______________________ muss ______________________

guess ______________________

II There is a pattern of words, nicknamed "ild, old words," in which the **i** or **o** is long /ī/, /ō/, as in **child, old**.

Exercise 3

Copy, saying the letters as you write them:

mild	______________	grind	______________
wild	______________	blind	______________
pint	______________	rind	______________
kind	______________	hind	______________
find	______________	mind	______________
wind	______________	bind	______________
cold	______________	sold	______________
gold	______________	scold	______________
fold	______________	told	______________
bold	______________	most	______________
hold	______________	post	______________
mold	______________	host	______________

III In a few words, the sound /u̇/ (**oo** as in **book**) is spelled with a **u**.

Exercise 4

Copy, repeating the letters:

put	______________	bushel	______________
puss	______________	pudding	______________

bush ______________________

push ______________________

butcher ______________________

bullet ______________________

pull ______________________

full ______________________

pulpit ______________________

painful ______________________

IV Sometimes the short sound of **u** /ŭ/ is spelled with the letter **o**, as in **mother**.

Exercise 5

Copy, saying the letters as you write them:

of ______________________

onion ______________________

oven ______________________

among ______________________

some ______________________

come ______________________

none ______________________

done ______________________

son ______________________

ton ______________________

won ______________________

honey ______________________

monkey ______________________

covey ______________________

Monday ______________________

month ______________________

front ______________________

nothing ______________________

sponge ______________________

tongue ______________________

cover ______________________

color ______________________

wonder	______________	comfort	______________
love	______________	other	______________
above	______________	brother	______________
shove	______________	govern	______________
glove	______________	dozen	______________
dove	______________	smother	______________
money	______________	London	______________

V Now and then the short sound of **u** /ŭ/ is spelled **ou**, as in **young**.

Exercise 6

Copy, saying the letters aloud:

country	______________	double	______________
couple	______________	trouble	______________
touch	______________	southern	______________

An easy way to remember most of these words is to learn this sentence: **The young country couple was touched with double trouble.**

Exercise 7

There are some vivid Anglo-Saxon words beginning with **gn**. Copy from the dictionary the ones you might find useful.

Composition 1

If you were running for mayor, what would you promise the voters to change in your town?

Composition 2

In buying a used car, what would you beware of?

The Spell of /ȯ/

THE SOUND of /Ȯ/

CHAPTER 10

Spelling the sound /ȯ/, as in **August**, can be complicated. Here are some hints:

I First, let us get **all** out of the way. These are simple words which you probably already know. They follow the **f**, **l**, **s** rule.

Exercise 1

Copy, repeating the letters as you write them:

all right	________	fall	________
ball	________	hall	________
call	________	small	________
wall	________	mall	________
tall	________	gall	________
stall	________		

Note: **already**, **although**, **always** and **almost** are single words; the expression **all right** is written as two words.

II /ȯ/ spelled **augh**. You will save yourself trouble by learning the sentences below:

The farmer caught his naughty daughter and taught her a lesson. Did he slaughter her?

The daughter was haughty as well as naughty.

Note: If you learn that **the boy was tough enough to be rough**, you will have three more words settled.

III /ȯ/ spelled **ough** as in **ought**.

Exercise 2

Copy, saying the letters as you write them:

ought	____________	sought	____________
bought	____________	nought	____________
brought	____________	thought	____________
fought	____________		

IV /ȯ/ spelled **au** or **aw**. The question is whether to use **au** or **aw**. Some of these choices are easy.

Use aw at the end of a word.

Exercise 3

Copy, saying the letters as you write them:

paw	____________	squaw	____________
jaw	____________	straw	____________
saw	____________	crawfish	____________

raw ______

claw ______

thaw ______

gnaw ______

drawer ______

outlaw ______

lawyer ______

Use aw in words of one syllable ending in l or n.

Exercise 4

Copy, saying the letters as you write them.

crawl ______

drawl ______

awl ______

scrawl ______

shawl ______

sprawl ______

bawl ______

brawl ______

yawl ______

lawn ______

dawn ______

yawn ______

pawn ______

spawn ______

prawn ______

drawn ______

brawn ______

Exceptions: haul, maul, Paul

There are five words that begin with aw:

awe
awful
awkward
awning
awl

Otherwise the sound /ȯ/ at the beginning of a word is spelled **au**.

Exercise 5

Copy, saying the letters as you write them.

author (ity)	__________	augment	__________
autumn	__________	August	__________
auction	__________	auspicious	__________
audit (ory)	__________	authentic	__________
audience	__________	auxiliary	__________
audacity	__________	austere	__________

Words beginning with **auto** (Greek - "self").

Exercise 6

Copy, saying the letters as you write them.

autobiography	__________	autopsy	__________
autocrat	__________	autograph	__________
automatic	__________	automobile	__________
autonomy	__________		

Exercise 7

Look up the derivation of these words beginning with **auto**. They are interesting.

____________________ ____________________

____________________ ____________________

____________________ ____________________

____

When the sound /ȯ/ occurs in the middle of a word, it is impossible to tell whether it is spelled **au** or **aw**. You will have to look it up. For your interest, here are some of these words:

hawk	haul	jaunt (y)	saucer
squawk	maul	saunter	nautical
hawser	laundry	daub	fraud (ulent)
dawdle	Paul	fault	tarpaulin
tawdry	(be) cause	vault	cauliflower
tawny	pause	laurel	mausoleum
hawthorn	haunch	pauper	laud (atory)
mawkish	haunt	applause	taut (ology)
trawler	daunt	caustic	bauble
	gaunt	faucet	

Composition 1

Describe Christmas from the point of view of a child.

Composition 2

Describe Christmas from the point of view of the cop on the beat.

Endings

OUS and US; FUL and LY;
IC and ICAL; CAL and CLE;
AL and EL

CHAPTER 11

OUS and US: Ous is an adjective ending. It can be attached to a noun according to the spelling rules:

marvel	marvelous
ruin	ruinous
joy	joyous
nerve	nervous
fame	famous
glory	glorious
victory	victorious

Exercise 1

Copy, saying each letter as you write it:

dangerous	____________________	contagious	____________________
humorous	____________________	infectious	____________________
libelous	____________________	mountainous	____________________
porous	____________________	courageous	____________________
perilous	____________________	outrageous	____________________
hazardous	____________________	miraculous	____________________
thunderous	____________________		

Us is a noun ending. There are more nouns ending in **us** in the word list section at the end of this book.

Exercise 2

Copy, saying each letter as you write it:

focus	____________	omnibus (bus)	____________
crocus	____________	census	____________
lotus	____________	radius	____________
exodus	____________	humus	____________
sinus	____________	fungus	____________
terminus	____________		

FUL and LY: You have already used the suffix **ful**. It is an adjective ending and makes an adjective out of a noun:

hope + ful hopeful
rest + ful restful

The word does not change. The **ful** is simply added to the root.

Exercise 3

Make adjectives out of these nouns by adding the suffix **ful**:

hate	**hateful**	spite	____________
help	____________	boast	____________
bliss	____________	fret	____________
sorrow	____________	law	____________

sin ______________________ bane ______________________

joy ______________________ mind ______________________

peace ______________________ harm ______________________

waste ______________________

Ly makes an adverb out of an adjective:

bad + ly badly
real + ly really
final + ly finally
hopeful + ly hopefully
restful + ly restfully

When **ly** is added to a word ending in **l**, it gives the effect of doubling. Now you know the logic behind the spelling of the word **really**.

When **ful** or **ly** is added to a word ending in **y**, naturally the Y Rule is followed:

ready + ly readily
duty + ful dutiful
play + ful playful

Exercise 4

Make adverbs out of the adjectives in Exercise 3 by adding **ly**:

______________________ ______________________ ______________________

______________________ ______________________ ______________________

______________________ ______________________ ______________________

______________________ ______________________ ______________________

______________________ ______________________ ______________________

Exercise 5

Make adjectives and adverbs out of the following nouns:

fancy	fanciful	fancifully
play	______	______
beauty	______	______
mercy	______	______
dread	______	______
tact	______	______
pain	______	______
use	______	______
pity	______	______
respect	______	______
health	______	______

Exercise 6

Make adverbs out of these adjectives:

punctual	punctually	healthy	______
busy	______	complete	______
sincere	______	usual	______
lucky	______	hurried	______
extreme	______	heavy	______

gentle + ly gently

When an adjective ends in **le**, drop the **le** and add **ly**, because it sounds better and is easier to say.

Exercise 7

Make adverbs out of these words:

simple + ly	**simply**	reliable + ly	______
double + ly	______	ample + ly	______
capable + ly	______	incredible + ly	______
feeble + ly	______	responsible + ly	______
single + ly	______	suitable + ly	______
probable + ly	______	sensible + ly	______

IC and ICAL: These are adjective endings.

Exercise 8

Make adjectives out of these nouns:

athlete	**athletic**	poet	______
history	______	hero	______
prophet	______	angel	______
period	______	chaos	______
democrat	______	cube	______
drama	______		

Exercise 9

Make adjectives out of these nouns by adding **ical**. Don't forget the spelling rules.

tact	**tactical**	symmetry	____________
method	____________	sphere	____________
cone	____________		

CAL and CLE: cal is an adjective ending; **cle** is a noun ending.

Exercise 10

Copy, saying the letters as you write them.

critical	____________	nautical	____________
logical	____________	theatrical	____________
classical	____________	magical	____________
tropical	____________	mechanical	____________
ethical	____________	statistical	____________
practical	____________	musical	____________
tactical	____________	physical	____________
clerical	____________	reciprocal	____________

Exercise 11

Copy, saying each letter as you write it.

miracle	________________	uncle	________________
article	________________	spectacle	________________
particle	________________	cubicle	________________
circle	________________	obstacle	________________
vehicle	________________	cuticle	________________
bicycle	________________		

Vowels in unstressed syllables are so slurred that it is often difficult to tell by the sound which vowel is being used. Sometimes another form of the word, in which the unstressed syllable becomes a stressed syllable, will tell you. For instance: **vehicle, vehicular; spectacle, spectacular; miracle, miraculous.** This is a very useful technique which should be remembered and employed whenever possible.

By analogy, note that **principal** is an adjective and **principle** is a noun: **The principal of a school is the principal officer. He had firm principles.**

AL and EL: Here are some generalizations that will help a little with these pesky endings. **Al** is an adjective ending. It can be added to Latin roots to form adjectives.

Exercise 12

Copy, saying the letters as you write them:

legal	________________	mental	________________
regal	________________	liberal	________________
annual	________________	literal	________________

perennial	________	cardinal	________
vocal	________	maternal	________
vital	________	paternal	________
rural	________	fraternal	________
frugal	________	capital*	________
brutal	________		

*The capital city of a state is the **capital**. The **capitol** in Washington is the building where Congress meets.

Al may be added to nouns to form adjectives.

Exercise 13

Form the adjectives, using the spelling rules:

universe	**universal**	orient	________
remedy	**remedial**	architecture	________
origin	________	department	________
nation	________	secretary	________
exception	________	structure	________
industry	________	territory	________
accident	________	testimony	________
occasion	________	fate	________

Al, unfortunately, can be a noun ending also. It may be added to verbs to form nouns.

Exercise 14

Form the nouns, using the spelling rules.

reverse + al	**reversal**	propose + al	________
try + al	**trial**	dispose + al	________
recite + al	________	rehearse + al	________
betray + al	________	renew + al	________
approve + al	________	acquit + al	________
deny + al	________		

El is usually a noun ending.

Exercise 15

Copy, saying each letter as you write it:

chapel	________	squirrel	________
model	________	quarrel	________
shovel	________	channel	________
bushel	________	barrel	________
panel	________	colonel	________
kennel	________	kernel	________
jewel	________	enamel	________
sequel	________	funnel	________

novel ____________________ label ____________________

travel ____________________ trowel ____________________

Exercise 16

Look up the words beginning with **kn** in the dictionary and copy the ones you think you might find useful.

Composition 1

Describe Christmas from the point of view of a store manager.

Composition 2

If you had a used car you wanted to sell, how would you go about selling it.

Plurals, Possessives, and Contractions

CHAPTER 12

Plurals:

I To form a plural (more than one) add s to a singular noun: **paper, papers, chair, chairs, window, windows.**

If you cannot hear the s as in words ending in **s, x, z, sh and ch,** add **es** instead: **ax, axes, class, classes, watch, watches.**

You know from the Y Rule that words ending in **y** preceded by a vowel do not change. The plural is formed as usual by adding **s**: **chimney, chimneys.**

Words ending in **y** preceded by a consonant change the **y** to **i** and add **es**: **city, cities.**

Exercise 1

Form the plural, saying the letters as you write them:

hobby	____________	fox	____________
mass	____________	loss	____________
table	____________	spy	____________
pulley	____________	marsh	____________
country	____________	patch	____________
annex	____________	box	____________
waltz	____________	coat	____________

joy ______________________

turkey ______________________

body ______________________

brush ______________________

key ______________________

toy ______________________

ray ______________________

candy ______________________

army ______________________

stitch ______________________

peach ______________________

II Most nouns ending in **f** or **fe** form the plural as usual by adding **s**: **roof, roofs, chief, chiefs.** A few change the **f** or **fe** into **ves**: **self, selves, life, lives.**

Exercise 2

Form the plural with **ves**:

shelf **shelves**

leaf ______________________

half ______________________

calf ______________________

loaf ______________________

thief ______________________

wolf ______________________

wife ______________________

knife ______________________

III Nouns ending in **o** after a vowel form the plural as usual by adding **s**: **radio, radios**.

Exercise 3

Form the plural:

studio	__________	trio	__________
cameo	__________	embryo	__________
taboo	__________	kangaroo	__________
curio	__________	portfolio	__________

IV Nouns ending in **o** that come from Spanish or Italian add **s** as usual to form the plural: **cello, cellos, burro, burros**. Look up other nouns ending in **o** after a consonant.

Exercise 4

Form the plural:

solo	solos	pinto	__________
alto	__________	bronco	__________
piano	__________	lasso	__________
soprano	__________	poncho	__________
libretto	__________	pueblo	__________
contralto	__________	sombrero	__________

Possessives: The idea of owning something is conveyed by the apostrophe. To form the possessive, first write the word. Then add an apostrophe. If the word does not end in s, add an s. Also, use the apostrophe to make the plural of letters and numbers: **7's, B's**.

table	table'	table's
	tables	tables'
child	child'	child's
children	children'	children's

Exception: proper names ending in s do add an s to form the possessive: **Mr. Jones's.**

Exercise 5

Give the singular (one) possessive, the plural, and the plural possessive:

Singular	**Singular Possessive**	**Plural**	**Plural Possessive**
boy	boy's	boys	boys'
church	church's	churches	churches'
lady	lady's	ladies	ladies'
window			
turkey			
loaf			
city			
man			
agency			
writer			
committee			

dentist	______	______	______
monkey	______	______	______
factory	______	______	______
thief	______	______	______
bush	______	______	______
chimney	______	______	______
daisy	______	______	______
lens	______	______	______
enemy	______	______	______
peach	______	______	______
lasso	______	______	______
chair	______	______	______
duty	______	______	______
torch	______	______	______
valley	______	______	______
penny	______	______	______
taxpayer	______	______	______

Fill in:

Singular	Singular Possessive	Plural	Plural Possessive
spray	________	________	________
copy	________	________	________
soprano	________	________	________
wife	________	________	________
pulley	________	________	________
book	________	________	________
march	________	________	________
story	________	________	________
leaf	________	________	________
woman	________	________	________
tax	________	________	________
dog	________	________	________
gypsy	________	________	________
alley	________	________	________
ally	________	________	________
hostess	________	________	________
witch	________	________	________

company	________	________	________
trolley	________	________	________
atlas	________	________	________
library	________	________	________

Contractions: We often slur words in English. When we slur to the extent of leaving out letters, we make ourselves respectable by inserting an apostrophe.

Exercise 7

Make the contractions:

You would	you'd	I have	________
do not	________	they are	________
we are	________	who is	________
I am	________	could not	________
would not	________	should have	________
she would	________	cannot	________
we will	________	I would	________
let us	________	they have	________
you are	________	It is	________

Exercise 8

There are some exciting words beginning with **wr**. Copy from the dictionary as many as you think might be useful.

Composition 1

Choose an editorial from any magazine or newspaper and write an essay from the opposite point of view.

Composition 2

How would you behave when being interviewed for a job? Think it over (dress, manner, past history, qualifications).

Ways of Spelling /ər/

CHAPTER 13

EAR: There are too many ways of spelling /ə r/, but a few generalizations help. Let's get rid of **ear** first.

Exercise 1

Copy, saying the words as you write them:

earn ______________________

learn ______________________

early ______________________

earnest ______________________

search ______________________

research ______________________

heard ______________________

pearl ______________________

hearse ______________________

rehearsal ______________________

earth ______________________

dearth ______________________

yearn ______________________

OUR: There are a few words, usually from the French, that spell /ər/ with **our**.

Exercise 2

Copy, saying the letters as you write them:

journey	________________	flourish	________________
journal	________________	courage	________________
adjourn	________________	courteous	________________
sojourn	________________	scourge	________________
		nourish	________________

ER

I Here is a sure thing: **er** is used as an ending in the comparative degree of adjectives – **bigger, colder, hotter, finer, happier, later**, etc.

Exercise 3

Make a list of a dozen adjectives in the comparative degree; that is, add **er** to the adjectives:

________________	________________	________________	________________
________________	________________	________________	________________
________________	________________	________________	________________

II **Er** is an ending meaning "one who," which is added to short Anglo-Saxon words and some others: **baker, teacher, runner, driver, swimmer.**

III **Er** is added to words to describe a person who lives in a certain place: **villager, southerner, islander, New Yorker, Londoner, foreigner.**

IV **Er** is the usual spelling of /ər/ in the middle of a word: **property, gallery, misery, several, energy, general, mineral, liberal.**

There are more **er** words in the word list section.

Exercise 4

There are some words from the Greek beginning with **rh**. Look them up in the dictionary and copy those you might find useful.

IR: More words have /ər/ spelled **ir** than are spelled **our** or **ear** as in the preceding lists. You will probably have to look them up. Below are some of them. You will find others in the word list section at the end of this book.

Exercise 5

Copy, saying the letters as you write them:

firm	______________	dirge	______________
confirm	______________	girdle	______________
squirm	______________	sirloin	______________
squirt	______________	virtue	______________
mirth	______________	skirmish	______________
flirt	______________	swirl	______________
whirl	______________	girth	______________
twirl	______________	squirrel	______________
birch	______________	hirsute	______________

UR: There are even more words spelled **ur** than are spelled **ir**. More **ur** words appear in the word list section.

Exercise 6

Copy, saying the letters as you write them:

curly	______________	purpose	______________
hurl	______________	surplus	______________
purse	______________	insurgent	______________
purple	______________	excursion	______________
church	______________	absurd	______________
turtle	______________	suburb	______________
nursery	______________	usurp	______________
surprise	______________	hurdle	______________
surge	______________	sturdy	______________
furnish	______________	spur	______________
furtive	______________	curt	______________
murder	______________		

OR

I Here is something dependable: the /ər/ sound after **w** is spelled **or**.

Exercise 7

Copy, saying the words as you write:

word	______________	worship	______________

worm	______	worth	______
world	______	worthy	______
work	______	worse	______
worry	______	worst	______

II **Or** may be added to verbs ending in **ate** to make nouns: **operate, operator.**

Exercise 8

Add **or**, using the Silent e Rule:

radiate	**radiator**	initiate	______
calculate	______	refrigerate	______
elevate	______	investigate	______
dictate	______	navigate	______
percolate	______	administrate	______
regulate	______	educate	______
translate	______	legislate	______
vibrate	______	illustrate	______
cultivate	______		

III Some abstract nouns end in **or.** This helps a little.

Exercise 9

Copy, saying the letters as you write:

humor	______________	terror	______________
honor	______________	vigor	______________
color	______________	glamor	______________
candor	______________	valor	______________
labor	______________	splendor	______________
favor	______________	major	______________
error	______________	minor	______________

IV **Or** may be attached to Latin roots, usually ending in **s** or **t**: **elect, elector, profess, professor.**

Exercise 10

Add **or**:

contract	______________	act	______________
invent	______________	collect	______________
inspect	______________	credit	______________
visit	______________	aggress	______________
audit	______________	distribute	______________
edit	______________	conduct	______________
assess	______________	instruct	______________

AR

I This you can count on: the suffix **ward** is spelled with **ar**—**inward, upward, westward, forward**.

II Some adjectives end in **ar**.

Exercise 11

Copy, saying the letters as you write it:

insular	________________	circular	________________
singular	________________	solar	________________
regular	________________	lunar	________________
familiar	________________	angular	________________
particular	________________	stellar	________________
polar	________________	muscular	________________
similar	________________	popular	________________
tubercular	________________	granular	________________

III Some words end in **ard.**

Exercise 12

Copy, saying the letters as you write:

standard	________________	blizzard	________________
custard	________________	sluggard	________________
mustard	________________	scabbard	________________

hazard	______	steward	______
coward	______	orchard	______
lizard	______	tankard	______
		wizard	______

IV Some nouns end in **ar**.

Exercise 13

Copy, saying the words as you write them:

scholar	______	vicar	______
beggar	______	grammar	______
liar	______	mortar	______
bursar	______	calendar	______
dollar	______	cellar	______
collar	______	nectar	______
hangar	______	nectarine	______
cedar	______		

Composition 1

Relate an incident that was embarrassing to you.

Composition 2

Describe a particular magazine, its purpose, kinds of articles, kinds of pictures, etc.

More Endings

TION and SION; CIAL, TIAL, and CIOUS; CIAN;
ANCE and ANT; ENCE and ENT;
ABLE and IBLE; ARY, ORY, and ERY

CHAPTER 14

TION: The sound /sh/ is spelled **ti** in **tion** /shun/.

Exercise 1

Copy, saying the letters as you write them:

notion	________	attention	________
lotion	________	collection	________
motion	________	emotion	________
nation	________	traction	________
station	________	immigration	________
friction	________	opposition	________
caution	________	fraction	________

SION: **sion** has the sound of /zhun/. If you listen carefully, you can tell whether to use **sion** or **tion** by the sound.

Exercise 2

Copy, saying each letter as you write it:

division	____________	occasion	____________
explosion	____________	abrasion	____________
excursion	____________	inclusion	____________
invasion	____________	version	____________
confusion	____________	precision	____________

Words with roots ending in **ss** have the **sion** spelling but the /shun/ sound. The word list section at the end of the book contains some of these words.

Exercise 3

List some words for each of these roots: **cess, press, gress, fess, miss, cuss.**

____________ ____________ ____________ ____________

____________ ____________ ____________ ____________

____________ ____________ ____________ ____________

____________ ____________ ____________ ____________

CIAL, TIAL, and CIOUS: **ous** and **al** are adjective endings you have met before. The **i** makes the **t** or **c** have a /sh/ sound.

To choose which to use, find a companion noun:

race	racial
space	spacious
confident	confidential
ferocity	ferocious

Exercise 4

Form the adjective by adding **cial, tial, or cious.** Remember to use the spelling rules.

face	____________	tenacity	____________
grace	____________	president	____________
finance	____________	commerce	____________
society	____________	resident	____________
atrocity	____________	glacier	____________

Exceptions:

benefit	beneficial (beneficent)
palace (Fr.)	palatial (Lat.)
space	spatial

CIAN: There is a group of words from the Greek, which end in **cian.**

Exercise 5

Copy, saying the letter as you write it:

magician	____________	technician	____________
physician	____________	musician	____________
optician	____________	electrician	____________
politician	____________		

ANCE and ANT; ENCE and ENT: A few principles help in choosing **ance** or **ence**.

Ant and Ance

I Use them if you can find a companion word ending in **ation**:

Companion Word	**Adjective**	**Noun**
domination	dominant	dominance
importation	important	importance
expectation	expectant	expectancy
variation	variant	variance

II Add **ance** to a verb to make a noun.

Exercise 6

guide	guidance	annoy	____________
appear	____________	acquaint	____________
rely	____________	comply	____________
defy	____________	contrive	____________
endure	____________	grieve	____________
ignore	____________	inherit	____________
observe	____________	insure	____________
perform	____________	persevere	____________
accord	____________	resist	____________
suffer	____________	assist	____________

III Add **ance**, instead of **ence**, to the root to keep **c and g** hard: **elegance, significance.**

There are three contractions:

hinder	hindrance
enter	entrance
remember	remembrance

IV Use **ant** for nouns meaning persons.

Exercise 7

Copy, saying the letters as you write them:

tenant	____________	occupant	____________
lieutenant	____________	accountant	____________
sergeant	____________	applicant	____________
defendant	____________	assailant	____________
descendant	____________	truant	____________
attendant	____________	inhabitant	____________

Exceptions:

superintendent
president
resident

Ent and Ence

I Use after a root ending in **i**.

Exercise 8

Copy, saying each letter as you write it:

audience	______________	ingredient	______________
experience	______________	incipient	______________
convenience	______________	lenient	______________
expedience	______________	efficient	______________
obedience	______________	ancient	______________
proficiency	______________	recipient	______________
sufficient	______________	patient	______________

Exceptions: radiant (radiation) and valiant

II After **qu**, use **ent** or **ence**:

eloquent	eloquence
consequent	consequence
delinquent	delinquency
frequent	frequency

III To keep **c and g** soft, use **ent** instead of **ant**:

innocent	stringent
magnificent	contingent
reticent	negligent
intelligent	diligent

IV Words ending in **escent**:

incandescent	convalescent	obsolescent
adolescent	quiescent	evanescent
flourescent	acquiescent	phosphorescent

V Some Latin roots take **ent** or **ence**:

FER* (bear)	**SIST** (stand)	**MIN** (jut)	**HER** (stick)
conference	subsistence	prominent	adherence
deference	persistence	imminent	coherence
difference	insistence	eminent	incoherent
preference	consistent		inherent
reference	existence	**CUR** (run)	
transference		occurrence	**SPOND** (pledge)
		recurrence	despondent
But: sufferance	**But**: assistance	concurrence	respondent
	resistance		correspondent

*When **fer** and **her** take **ence** the **r** is not doubled.
Note: We have been dealing with an **ending** spelled **ence**. The same sound in the body of a word is usually spelled **ense**, as in **tense, dense, sense, intense, expense, immense.**

ABLE and IBLE: How do you decide which of these endings to use? You already know some ways.

I Be consistent. If you use **ance** and **ation** with a word, you naturally use **able**.

Exercise 9

Form the companion adjective, using **able**:

taxation	taxable	variation	________
admiration	________	application	________
dispensation	________	operation	________
duration	________	education	________
adaptation	________	communication	________
imagination	________		

II Use **able** to turn a verb into an adjective. This is a very useful suggestion, as there are a great many of these words.

Exercise 10

Turn these verbs into adjectives, using the spelling rules:

live	**livable**	like	______
pity	**pitiable**	notice	______
vary	______	compare	______
justify	______	conceive	______
prefer	______	note	______
profit	______	advise	______
recognize	______	cure	______
rely	______	deny	______
use	______	manage	______

III If a companion word ends in **tion** or **sion**, use **ible**.

Exercise 11

Form the companion adjective, using **ible**:

destruction	**destructible**	digestion	______
perception	______	comprehension	______
division	______	admission	______
accession	______	deduction	______

permission	________	reversion	________
audition	________	collection	________
combustion	________		

IV Use **ible** to keep **c** and **g** soft.

Exercise 12

Copy, saying each letter as you write it:

forcible	________	invincible	________
tangible	________	negligible	________
legible	________	incorrigible	________
reducible	________	crucible	________
eligible	________		

ARY, ORY, and ERY: Which should you use? You can usually tell by the sound, especially if the **ar** or **or** is an accented syllable. **Er** is usually not accented, but in general is used in words pertaining to an occupation.

Exercise 13

Copy, saying the letters as you write them:

literary	________	vocabulary	________
January	________	voluntary	________
stationary	________	secondary	________
temporary	________	tributary	________

contemporary ________________ salary ________________

arbitrary ________________ contrary ________________

dietary ________________ primary ________________

infirmary ________________ secretary ________________

imaginary ________________

Exercise 14

Copy, saying each letter as you write it:

theory ________________ dormitory ________________

contributory ________________ explanatory ________________

migratory ________________ introductory ________________

satisfactory ________________ memory ________________

advisory ________________ victory ________________

factory ________________ oratory ________________

directory ________________ exclamatory ________________

compulsory ________________ conservatory ________________

accessory ________________

Exercise 15

Copy, saying each letter as you write it:

nursery	____________	archery	____________
creamery	____________	gunnery	____________
pottery	____________	hatchery	____________
bakery	____________	distillery	____________
misery	____________	drapery	____________
refinery	____________	stationery	____________
machinery	____________	artillery	____________
celery	____________	cutlery	____________

Composition 1

Describe a day on the water.

Composition 2

Enlarge on this quotation: "Wit has truth in it; wisecracking is simply calisthenics with words."*

Dorothy Parker

**Bartlett's Familiar Quotations*, by John Bartlett, Little, Brown and Co., Boston, Massachusetts.

Greek Prefixes

CHAPTER 15

For the student who likes words here are some Greek prefixes. These are easy to look up because most of them are bunched in the dictionary. Try it. The derivations are fascinating.

a	*not, without,*	anhydrous	asexual
an before vowel or h	*negative*	anomalous	amorphous
		anonymous	anarchy
		apathy	amethyst
		aphasia	amnesty
		atheist	anesthesia
		amoral	aneroid
		anecdote	asymmetric
		anemia	alexia
		abyss	adamant
		agnostic	analgesic
acro	*highest,*	acrobat	acropolis
	outermost	acronym	acrostic
allo	*other*	allergy	allegory
amphi	*both, about,*	amphibious	amphitheater
	around	amphipod	amphora
ana	*up, upward,*	analogy	anathema
	back, again	anatomy	analysis
		anachronism	anode
		anagram	

anti **ant** before a vowel	*opposite,* *against*	antidote antarctic antigen antiphony antithesis antonym	antagonize antibiotic anthem antiseptic antipathy
apo **ap** before a vowel **aph** before an aspirate	*off, from,* *away from*	apostasy apocalypse apocrypha apology apoplexy apostle	apostrophe apothecary aphasia aphorism apogee
archi **arch**	*chief, principal*	archangel architect	archipelago archetype
caco	*bad, ill*	cacophony cacography	cacodyl
cata **cat** before vowel **cath** before aspirate	*down, away,* *completely* *against*	category cataclysm catalogue catalepsy catastrophe catapult cathode	catholic cataract catalyst catarrh catatonic catechism
di **dis**	*two-fold,* *double*	diploma diphthong	dilemma diptych
dia **di**	*through, apart,* *across* *thoroughly*	diameter diagonal diagram diaphonous diadem diatribe	diagnose diaphragm diastole dialogue diocese diorama
dys	*bad, ill, hard* *(opposite of* **eu***)*	dyslexia dysgenic dystrophe	dyspepsia dysentery dysfunction

en **el** before l **em** before b, m, p, ph	*in*	endemic energetic encyclical ellipsis embolism encomium	emphasis embryo empathy empirical empyrean
endo	*within*	endochrome endocardial	endocrine endogamy
epi **ep** before vowel **eph** before aspirate	*upon, on, above, over, among*	epidemic epitaph epithet ephemeral epidermis	epilepsy episode epistle epitome epigram
eu	*well, good, (opposite of* **dys** *and* **caco***)*	eulogy euphony eugenics eunuch	euphemism euphoric euthanasia
hemi	*half*	hemisphere hemicycle	hemiplegia
hetero	*another, different*	heterodox heterogenous	heteronym heterosexual
homo	*same, like, equal*	homogeneous	homonym
hydro **hydra** before vowel	*water*	hydroplane hydraulic hydrant hydroelectric	hydrogen hydrophobia hydrometer
hyper	*over, above, excessive*	hyperactive hypercritical	hyperbole
hypo	*under, beneath, slightly*	hypodermic hypotenuse hyphen	hypocrisy hypostasize hypochondria

mega	*great, large*	megalopolis megalomania megaphone	megacycle megaton
meta **met** before vowel **meth** before aspirate	*with, after,* *over,* *beyond*	metaphor metaphysical method	metabolism metamorphosis metastasis
micro	*small*	microbe microscope microcosm	microphone Micronesia
mono **mon** before vowel	*one, single,* *alone*	monograph monologue monarch monocle monolithic monopoly monorail	monoplane monogamy monochrome monogram monotone monotony
neo	*new, recent*	neolithic neophyte	neologism neon
ortho **orth** before vowel	*right, correct,* *straight*	orthography orthodox orthopedic	orthoptics orthodontics
pan, panto	*all*	panorama pantheon panacea pancreas	panoply pantheism pantomine pandemonium
para **par** before vowel	*beside, beyond,* *amiss, contrary*	parable paradox parasite parody parabola paradise paragon parapsychology	parapet paragraph parallel paralysis paraphernalia paranoid paraphrase paraplegic

peri	*around, about, near*	periodic perimeter perigee	periphery periscope peripatetic
phono	*sound*	phonograph phonology phonetic	phonic phonogram
photo	*light*	photography photoelectric photogenic	photosynthesis photo finish photostat
poly	*many*	polygamy polysyllable polyglot	Polynesia polyandrous polygyny
pro	*before, for*	prologue prophet proboscis program	protagonist proscenium prognathous
pros	*to, toward*	prosody proselyte	prosthesis
proto	*first, primary*	protocol prototype protozoa	protagonist protoplasm
pseudo	*false, fictitious*	pseudonym	
psycho	*relating to soul or mind*	psychology psychometry psychiatry psychic	psychopath psychosis psychosomatic psychotherapy
syn **sy** before s, z **syl** before l **sym** before b, m, & p	*with, together*	synopsis syntax system syllable symbol symmetry sympathy	symphony symposium symptom synagogue synchronize syndicate syndrome

Review Exercises

CHAPTER 16

One of the ten words on each list is correct. Proofread the words and spell them properly:

Exercise 1

scrach	____________	buge	____________
merrely	____________	craftyness	____________
bigest	____________	freind	____________
standing	____________	timming	____________
hopful	____________	arguement	____________

Exercise 2

swiming	____________	furyous	____________
takeing	____________	doge	____________
lonly	____________	truely	____________
farming	____________	noisless	____________
sliegh	____________	fech	____________

Exercise 3

hazy	____________	losion	____________
operater	____________	conferrence	____________
distillary	____________	studyous	____________
performence	____________	changable	____________
recitle	____________	droping	____________

Exercise 4

tirless	____________	obediance	____________
percieve	____________	partical	____________
sufering	____________	humorus	____________
preceed	____________	luner	____________
acommodate	____________	weird	____________

Exercise 5

accurred	____________	unforgetable	____________
interceed	____________	sandwitch	____________
prefered	____________	greaving	____________
pulleys	____________	liklihood	____________
interupted	____________	accross	____________

Composition 1

Look up these words in **Roget's Thesaurus** and use a synonym for each in a sentence. If you can make a connected story of them, please do:

moldy	joy
intuition	wordy
spy	chubby
insanity	

Composition 2

Enlarge on this quotation: "Let there be spaces in your togetherness."*

Kahlil Gibran

**The Shorter Bartlett's Familiar Quotations* A Permabook Edition, Pocket Books, Inc., New York, New York.

Word Lists

CHAPTER 17

Nouns ending in us

typhus
hibiscus
papyrus
colossus
octopus
hippopotamus

Adjectives ending in ous

odorous
traitorous
vaporous
clamorous
villainous
lustrous
tremulous
monstrous
wondrous
fabulous
mischievous

nebulous
ominous
chivalrous
hideous
extraneous
erroneous
spontaneous
simultaneous
courteous
miscellaneous
odious

curious
previous
religious
laborious
imperious
fastidious
hilarious
cautious
ambitious
circuitous
illustrious

nutritious
suspicious
superstitious
conspicuous
continuous
impetuous
tumultuous
virtuous
deciduous
incongruous

Tion words /shŭn/

mention
persecution
commotion
expedition

execution
devotion
preposition
appreciation

proposition
diction
proportion

Sion words /zhŭn/

fusion
collusion
erosion
perversion

exclusion
derision
profusion
seclusion

provision
persuasion
revision
elision

Sion /shŭn/ in words with a root ending in ss:

expression
oppression
impression
depression
compression
suppression
repression

digression
progression
transgression

congressional

concession
procession
intercession
recession
succession
secession

profession
confession

discussion

concussion
percussion

mission
permission
commission
admission
submission
intermission
transmission

possession

Also:
compulsion
expulsion
propulsion

comprehension
apprehension

convulsion
revulsion

extension
pretension

The /sh/ sound, spelled ch; generally from the French

cliché
cache
chute
chateau

champagne
chandelier
chivalry
brochure

machine
mustache
Chicago
gauche

ei as /ē/
weir
inveigle
seigneur

ei as /ĕ/
nonpareil

ei as /ā/
seine
geisha
peignoir
surveillance
obeisance
inveigh
heinous

ei as /ī/
seismic
seismograph
gneiss
leitmotiv
kaleidoscope
sleight of hand
eiderdown

ie as /ē/
lief
mien
frieze
liege
fief
cavalier
chandelier
cashier

Words ending in age

bandage
package
manage
damage
savage
voltage
village

message
garbage
advantage
baggage
luggage
postage
cottage

coinage
tonnage
shortage
forage
cribbage
wreckage
carnage

silage
vintage
mileage
spoilage
poundage
pillage
average

Words ending in ture

moisture
lecture
fracture
adventure
picture
future
mixture
nature
pasture

nurture
architecture
fixture
departure
miniature
imposture
structure
culture

stricture
agriculture
scripture
temperature
puncture
capture
ligature
literature

torture
feature
legislature
manufacture
furniture
mature
century

saturate

Ea as /ā/

break
great
steak
bear
pear
tear
wear
yea

Ea as /ē/

sea
tea
flea
each
beach
peach
reach
teach
bead
lead
read
leaf
leak
beak
peak
speak
weak
streak
sneak
squeak
heal
meal
squeal
steal
beam
seam
team
steam
stream
dream
bean
lean
mean
clean
heap
leap
cheap
reap
ear
fear
hear
near
tear
dear
clear
shear
ease
easy
tease
please
feat
east
beast
feast
yeast
eat
beat
heat
meat
neat
seat
cheat
treat
wheat
eaves
leave
teamster
appeal
conceal
reveal
repeat
retreat
defeat
increase
release
eagle
eager
beaver
reason
creature
heathen
meager
measles
peacock
peanut
weave
year
seal

Ea as /ĕ/

head
dead
lead
read (y)
dread
bread (th)
spread
(in) stead (y)
thread
deaf
breast
health (y)
wealth
stealth
meant
heavy
sweat (er)
breath
meadow
tread
dealt
death
realm
weapon
treadle
heaven
pleasant
measure
treasure
feather
heather
leather
weather

tee	reef	deep	squeeze
see	seek	keep	kneel
fee	week	sheep	cheese
bee	cheek	steep	seethe
flee	creek	sweep	tweezers
free	peek	creep	proceed
glee	leek	peep	canteen
three	meek	sleep	tureen
tree	eel	deer	agree
beech	feel	cheer	decree
leech	heel	queer	pedigree
speech	keel	beet	referee
screech	peel	feet	refugee
deed	reel	meet	nominee
feed	steel	sheet	employee
need	seem	sweet	feeble
seed	seen	street	peevish
weed	screen	fleet	peerage
bleed	keen	greet	career
reed	queen	breeze	engineer
greed	green	freeze	volunteer
beef	sheen	sneeze	domineer

Words ending in ey

money	alley	donkey	medley
honey	attorney	turkey	abbey
chimney	kidney	volley	galley
monkey	whiskey	trolley	hackney
valley	jockey	journey	key
pulley	barley	hockey	jersey
			covey

<u>Oi</u> and <u>oy</u>

Very few words begin with this sound:

oil	ointment	oyster

Inside a word, **oi** is more common than **oy**, especially in words of one syllable. At the end of a word, the sound is spelled **oy**.

soil	joist	destroy	toy
toil	hoist	corduroy	joy
coil	anoint	voyage	coy
boil	rejoice	loyal	boy
spoil	poison	royal	soybean
coin	exploit	arroyo	cloy
join	thyroid	boycott	decoy
joint	adenoid	gargoyle	annoy
point	embroider	flamboyant	deploy
moisture	boisterous	clairvoyant	employ
noisy	poinsettia		
avoid			

<u>Ou</u> and <u>ow</u>

At the end of a word, the sound is spelled **ow**. Otherwise you will have to look up the spelling or memorize it. If a word of one syllable ends in **l** or **n**, the sound is usually spelled **ow**.

vouch	sprout	growl	trowel
pouch	trout	scowl	allow
pound	south	brow	flower
abound	mouth	plow	rowdy
proud	ounce	frown	dower
cloud	flounce	crown	prowess
scour	surround	crowd	howitzer
flour	county	drowsy	dowager
grouse	thousand	towel	endowment
mouse	scoundrel		

More ir words

bird
chirp
girl
first
skirt

stir
dirt
shirt

birthday
fir
third
thirty

circle
sir
thirsty
dirk

More ur words

bur
fur
blur
urge
nurse
churn
burn
further
turn

Thursday
Saturday
furl
surf
spurn
lurk
curfew
gurgle

turban
refurbish
disturbance
regurgitate
diurnal
nocturnal
nasturtium
metallurgy

occurrence (the root **cur**)
perturb
pursue
surpass (the prefix **super**)
surmount
survive
auburn
sulphur

More er words

her
were
jerk
nervous
perch
fern
verse
stern
term
sister
serve

servant
herd
sermon
fertile
berg
berth
germinate
serf
merge
serge
verge

terse
certify
dervish
hermit
kernel
mercy
pergola
serpent
sterling
termite
thermal

verdict
internal
commercial
preferment (the root **fer**)
diversion
imperfect (the prefix **per**)
reversal
exterminate
assertion
aspersion
concern

tea, tee
steal, steel
meat, meet, mete
beat, beet
beach, beech
creak, creek
sea, see
weak, week
peak, peek
heal, heel
seam, seem
peal, peel
leak, leek
read, reed
shear, sheer

team, teem
feat, feet
cheap, cheep
dear, deer

bare, bear
pare, pear, pair
brake, break
stake, steak
grate, great
ware, wear

plain, plane
main, mane
mail, male

pail, pale
pain, pane
sail, sale
tail, tale
hail, hale
ail, ale
maid, made
lain, lane
fair, fare
hair, hare
bail, bale
gait, gate
bait, bate
stair, stare

---

air, heir
aisle, isle
all, awl
allowed, aloud
altar, alter
arc, ark
ascent, assent
ball, bawl
base, bass
be, bee
beer, bier
bell, belle
berry, bury
berth, birth
blew, blue
board, bored
bolder, boulder
bough, bow
bread, bred
bridal, bridle
canvas, canvass
capital, capitol
cast, caste
cellar, seller

choir, quire
clause, claws
chord, cord
core, corps
coarse, course
cue, queue
dam, damn
die, dye
done, dun
dough, doe
dew, due
dual, duel
earn, urn
ate, eight
faint, feint
faun, fawn
fane, fain, feign
flea, flee
flew, flue
fort, forte,
foul, fowl
forth, fourth
fir, fur
gamble, gambol

gild, guild
gilt, guilt
hall, haul
heard, herd
hart, heart
hear, here
hoard, horde
hour, our
hew, hue
idle, idol
its, it's
lead, led
lessen, lesson
liar, lyre
loan, lone
load, lode
mantel, mantle
maze, maize
metal, mettle
miner, minor
naval, navel
knead, need
knight, night
none, nun

knot, not
one, won
passed, past
pedal, peddle
peer, pier
peace, piece
poll, pole
pore, pour
pray, prey
rain, reign, rein
raise, raze
read, red
rest, wrest
right, rite, wright, write
ring, wring
road, rode, rowed
roll, role
root, route

roe, row
scene, seen
cents, sense
shone, shown
cite, sight, site
slay, sleigh
sole, soul
some, sum
son, sun
soar, sore
sew, so, sow
staid, stayed
straight, strait
taught, taut
tear, tier
their, there, they're
threw, through
throne, thrown

to, too, two
toe, tow
tern, turn
vane, vain, vein
vale, veil
wait, weight
waist, waste
waive, wave
way, weigh
whole, hole
whose, who's
wood, would
wretch, retch
wrote, rote
yolk, yoke
yew, you, ewe
your, you're

Nonsense syllables: short vowels

das	sug	peb	lig
zin	hep	rom	rol
hom	fol	vix	vap
hab	quin	min	ket
bix	dos	peb	nal
jal	yid	dib	quib
dem	ron	dal	rel
vol	fif	vit	fis
des	zon	heb	pam
nup	daf	bez	pid
lis	ros	hos	nim
muz	saf	siz	jus
med	dus	quiv	wiz
kem	deg	fas	ped
jit	tet	sud	bak
mon	sym	gav	nov
dis	beb	pif	gat
wob	biv	rus	len
kel	reg	lav	zep
pud	yat	sep	gog

hild	scond	nade	pede
flab	sote	sniv	glit
cren	lusk	lect	flod
pute	stig	vive	fract
smol	rene	jole	bine
dult	nide	pleb	tate
vene	zond	brev	trib
grap	glox	griz	blad
spond	prof	quent	zome
fite	buke	labe	swiv
nate	broc	sliv	mide
grif	stant	hume	snaf
plim	tave	brun	fute
drant	reft	rupt	sade
nist	trast	dyte	nect
voke	prob	drog	strunt
clin	nize	sorp	gramp
fraz	cremp	flam	slasp
lete			

Composition 1

Enlarge on this quotation: "No one can make you feel inferior without your consent."*
—Eleanor Roosevelt

Composition 2

Enlarge on this quotation: "Injustice anywhere is a threat to justice everywhere."*
—Martin Luther King, Jr.

**Bartlett's Familiar Quotations*, by John Bartlett, Little, Brown and Co., Boston, Massachusetts.

The Phonograms

a says	ă as in apple, ā as in baby, ȯ as in all, ä as in father.
e says	ĕ as in elephant, ē as in recent.
i says	ĭ as in it, ī as in spider.
y says	ĭ as in gym, ī as in my or cyclone, ē as in candy.
o says	ŏ as in olive, ō as in pony, ŭ or ə as in mother.
u says	ŭ as in umbrella, yü as in music, ü as in ruby, u̇ as in push.

ai says	ā as in sail.
ay says	ā as in play.
ar says	**är** as in car.
au says	ȯ as in August.
aw says	ȯ as in saw.

---

a – e says	ā as in safe.
e – e says	ē as in these.
i – e says	ī as in pine.
y – e says	ī as in type.
o – e says	ō as in home.
u – e says	yü as in mule, ü as in rule.

---

ea says	ē as in eat, ĕ as in bread, ā as in steak.
ee says	ē as in feed.
ei says	ē as in ceiling, ā as in vein.
ey says	ē as in valley, ā as in they.
eigh says	ā as in eight.
ew says	yü as in few, ü as in grew.

oa says ō as in boat.

oe says ō as in toe.

oi says **ȯi** as in boil.

oy says **ȯi** as in toy.

oo says **ü** as in food,
u̇ as in book.

or says **ȯr** as in hornet.

ou says **au̇** as in out,
ü as in soup.

ow says **au̇** as in cow,
ō as in snow.

---

ue says **yü** as in rescue,
ü as in true.

er says **ər** as in her.

ir says **ər** as in bird.

ur says **ər** as in burn.

---

c says **k** as in cat,
s as in city
(before e, i, or y.)

---

g says **g** as in go,
j as in gym
(before e, i, or y.)

ĕd says **ĕd** as in rented,
d as in sailed,
t as in jumped.